THE HOUSE
THAT JESUS BUILT

'In an age where everyone is offering to re-design the church, Ralph Davis, in this small booklet, winsomely, clearly and most of all Biblically reminds us that we have a designer of the church – Jesus Christ – and the glory and majesty of His design. This is a great instrument to remind, encourage and attract people to the bride of Christ and the body of Christ – His Church.'

Harry L Reeder III,
Briarwood Presbyterian Church, Birmingham, Alabama

'Ralph Davis is a good friend, and a great bible teacher. He has endeared himself to bible readers everywhere through his books, and has probably done more to give real practical help in preaching the former prophets (Joshua – 2 Kings) than anyone else alive. Once again he has come up with a gem for us with this little manual on the church. Biblical, succinct, clear, fun and, above all, brief, I can't imagine anything better for teaching what it means to belong to 'The House that Jesus Built' – to new Christians who don't yet understand the church (and older ones who ought to!)'

William J U Philip,
St George's-Tron Church, Glasgow, Scotland

'This is a short book to give to visitors who may come to your church. In a very friendly, succinct and even fun way, it explains both the gospel and what it is to be a Christian and belong to a church shaped by a reformation approach to Scripture. It is a kind of brochure-cum-browser which enables people to make an informed choice about whether or not yours might be the church in which to settle. The brief explanations of the gospel are miniature masterpieces, which caused my heart to leap with thankfulness to God as I read them. Ralph Davis is not only a great expositor, he is also a winsome apologist for Reformation Christianity and this book will dissolve the prejudices which many people bring through our church doors and win them for Christ and his church.'

John Benton,
Evangelicals Now

THE HOUSE
THAT JESUS BUILT

Dale Ralph Davis

*An Introductory manual
about the church*

CHRISTIAN
FOCUS

Dale Ralph Davis is pastor of Woodland Presbyterian Church, Hattiesburg, Mississippi. Previously he taught Old Testament at Reformed Theological Seminary, Jackson, Mississippi. He has also written commentaries on:

Joshua (ISBN 978-1-84550-137-2)
Judges (ISBN 978-1-84550-138-9)
1 Samuel (ISBN 978-1-85792-516-6)
2 Samuel (ISBN 978-1-84550-270-6)
1 Kings (ISBN 978-1-84550-251-5)
2 Kings (ISBN 978-1-84550-096-2).

ISBN 1-84550-312-0
ISBN 978-1-84550-312-3

10 9 8 7 6 5 4 3 2 1

First edition published in 2007
(ISBN 1-84550-226-4 / ISBN 978-1-84550-226-3)
Revised edition published in 2007
by
Christian Focus Publications Ltd,
Geanies House, Fearn, Ross-shire,
IV20 1TW, Scotland, Great Britain
www.christianfocus.com

Cover design by Danie Van Straaten

Printed by Nørhaven Paperback A/S, Denmark

CONTENTS

NOTE FROM THE AUTHOR

When I get airline tickets I always go through a travel agent, even in this day of high-tech online purchasing options. Before I talk to my travel agent, however, I get on the internet and check various flight connections and prices. When I call my agent I may ask for a connection I had seen online. (I know I'd save money to purchase online – I simply have a psychological block about it.) I like to have a feel for my options before I talk to the agent. This book is something like that – in case you have some interest in joining a Reformed church it will give you an opportunity to see what it's like, or what it tries to be like. Hopefully, it will answer some of your questions.

I originally pulled together this material for visitors to our church – folks who are often curious and occasionally apprehensive about what the church is 'like.' Not many people come sliding out of a 'reformed' pipeline into a congregation. They come from all over the religious – and non-religious – spectrum. We don't want them to be surprised in a bad way about what they'll meet; hence this briefing.

And I must beg some charity. This tiny tome was written with a Presbyterian as the sample church. I can't much help being Presbyterian just now (they pay me, after all), but please know that I'm not assuming only Presbyterians are reformed. Happily, many Anglicans, Baptists, and others would place themselves under the reformed banner. Please understand that the Presbyterian particulars (e.g. the Westminster Confession) are intended as descriptive not pre-scriptive, as exemplary (that's the case in our church) not mandatory (what should be so in all reformed fellowships).

Ralph Davis
Woodland Presbyterian Church
Hattiesburg

WHAT OUR CHURCH BELIEVES 1

Don't swallow too hard. When we refer to what 'our church' believes you must realize that we are speaking loosely. It is hardly 'our church'; it is, we trust, Christ's church. When we call it 'our' church that is just a sloppy way of speaking about it among ourselves.

Sometimes people think churches like ours are 'different' because of what we believe. All depends on how you look at it. We are a confessional church, that is, we hold to a particular summary of biblical doctrine, namely the *Westminster Confession of Faith* plus the Larger and Shorter Catechisms. We do not put this confession of faith in place of the Bible. The Bible must hold supreme place for what the Christian believes; we only say that we believe the Westminster standards (as they are called) are a true and accurate summary of what the Bible teaches.

But I don't want to take you through the *Westminster Confession* right now. Sometimes a succinct digest, a brief outline of a church's doctrine, can give you a better flavor of the animal than a whole mass of details. So what follows is a sketch of our most distinctive beliefs. I support each of them from the life and teaching of Jesus, not because Jesus' teaching is 'better' than the rest of the Bible and not because I don't believe the rest of the Bible (for I do). But there's method along with madness here. You see, some people sometimes hear our church doctrines and they say (or think), 'Oh, that's what that rascal Paul taught – you know, Paul, the guy who took the nice, simple teachings of Jesus and screwed them up.' Now, I don't share that attitude for a second. But, for the sake of argument, I want to show that if anyone doesn't like the following teachings they have no one to blame but Jesus himself! And if someone doesn't believe what Jesus says, he or she shouldn't join his church.

Now, to the teaching.

The Bible is entirely true

Jesus' scripture was the Old Testament. According to Jesus, 'the Scripture cannot be broken' (that is, it cannot be emptied of its force by being proven false; John 10:35). For him, whatever Scripture says, God says (Matt. 15:4). And what God says is truth (John 17:17). Jesus wasn't simply saying nice things about the scriptures; he lived under their authority. He repelled Satan's temptations because he remained obedient to God's word – you may remember how three times he opposed Satan with 'it is written' (Matt. 4:4, 7, 10).

If we are faithful to Christ, our church must hold a very 'high' view of the Bible. He calls us to believe and obey what it says – even when it's not to our liking. A number of us have been in churches that have abandoned their belief in the entire trustworthiness of the Bible. When that is done, the church's foundations will crumble (eventually, if not sooner). If we can pick and choose what we will accept or reject from the Bible, then *we* have become the authority rather than holding the Bible as our authority. Then we have placed ourselves above God's word rather than under it.

Sinners are perfectly sinful

Now by this we do not mean no one ever does anything decent, or just, or moral, or kind; we don't mean every person is absolutely as evil in every way as he or she can possibly be (even society wouldn't usually allow that). But we mean every person is a sinner at the core of his or her being and that, apart from Christ, sin rules his perspectives, motives, desires, purposes. We might think Jesus would think more positively. But he said in teaching his disciples, 'If you, then, being evil, know how to give good gifts to your children...' (Matt. 7:11). And that is all the more powerful because Jesus was not directly teaching about our nature there; he was teaching about another topic and he merely makes this aside; he simply reveals the assumption he makes about human nature, as though he takes it for granted and above argument. 'If you, then, being evil...'

Maybe we prefer something more direct. Another time Jesus taught: 'For from within, out of men's hearts, come evil thoughts, sexual immorality, theft, murder, adultery, greed, malice, deceit, lewdness, envy, slander, arrogance and folly. All these evils come from inside and make a man unclean' (Mark 7:21-3). If we take Jesus seriously, the ruck and muck that we feel, think, and do will never surprise us. If we have a high view of the Bible, we should have a low view of ourselves as sinners apart from God's grace.

Many probably hold the view that 'I sin, therefore I am a sinner.' That is, my act of sinning makes me a sinner. But that is not what Jesus says in Mark 7. 'From within, out of men's hearts…' That is, our corrupt nature gives rise to the whole array of sinful acts. In short, 'I am a sinner, therefore I sin.' I am perverse at the core of my being and that gives rise to all sorts of evil.

God is really big

We believe – would that we really believed it as we should – that God is really big. (We hold with all Christians that there is one God and that he has revealed himself as triune, that is, that the Father, the Son, and the Holy Spirit is each fully and eternally God.) When we say God is really big, we mean he is 'sovereign,' that all things are under his sway – even falling sparrows (Matt. 10:29). But more, we believe God is so big that we would never come to Jesus in faith unless he brought us and made us able to come. You'd think we were helpless, huh? True, says Jesus, for 'no one is able to come to me unless the Father who sent me draws him' (John 6:44). It is those whom the Father gives to Jesus who will come to Jesus (John 6:37). People do not come to Jesus because they think it's a good idea. If any of us ever trusts in Jesus it is only because the Father gives us to Jesus and brings us to Jesus. That offends many people. They fight the idea that even our faith must be a gift of God (cf. Phil. 1:29). We can only say: Argue with Jesus – he's the one who said it.

The cross is absolutely central

Here we are at the heart of the gospel. Jesus said that his death was the reason he came: 'For even the Son of Man did not come to be served, but to serve, and to give his life a ransom for many' (Mark 10:45). We are held as captives of sin, and Jesus' death was the ransom-price that bought our release from that bondage.

You have a picture of what Jesus' death should mean for every Christian in Matthew 27:15-26 (it has been called 'the Barabbas theory of the atonement'). Barabbas was the one who should have died, raunchy villain and vicious criminal that he was; yet Barabbas is released and Jesus is crucified. If Barabbas ever heard of that, he should have realized that Jesus took his place, that Jesus died for him. That is what every Christian says about his Savior: I should have died; but Jesus took my place – Jesus died for me.

Grace is utterly incredible

Ask a Christian why God would send Christ to die for him, why God would draw him to believe in Jesus who died for him, why God would care a wink about someone who is evil at the core of his being, not to mention his overt acts – ask a Christian that, and if he's got his head screwed on straight that Wednesday, he'll simply smile and exclaim, 'I haven't the foggiest idea! It doesn't make sense, does it?' That a holy

God would give a moment's thought to sleazy sinners is beyond belief.

But God is not conventional. Grace is his biggest surprise. Why would anyone care about a woman of the streets having forgiveness of sins (Luke 7:36-50)? What father in his just and holy mind would wrap his arms around a stinking prodigal (Luke 15)? Who would dare teach that a cheating tax collector stood uncondemned before heaven (Luke 18:9-14)? Who would assure a condemned criminal within a gasp of his death that he would be in paradise that day (Luke 23:39-43)? There is no explanation, except: that's the way God is; that's the way Jesus delights to be. We hope that in our fellowship we can help people to be repeatedly flabbergasted at the grace of God.

Disciples are continually secure

We believe that once God brings a sinner to Jesus, Jesus will keep him to the end. This doesn't mean that the disciple will never sin or that he will never have temptations or endure hard afflictions or that he will never doubt his faith. But it does mean: 'All that the Father gives me will come to me, and whoever comes to me I will never drive away. For I have come down from heaven not to do my own will but to do the will of him who sent me. And this is the will of him who sent me, that I shall lose none of all that he has given me, but raise them up at the last day' (John 6:37-9). Or to put it in sheep language: 'My sheep listen to my voice; I know them, and they follow me. I give them eternal life, and they shall never perish; no one can snatch them out of my hand' (John 10:27-8). Jesus wants his people to know that they are secure in the grip of the strong Son of God. And we believe that.

Life is wholly holy

Once when Jesus had cast demons out of a man and made him completely whole, that man wanted to go with Jesus. But Jesus had other plans for him: 'Go home to your family and tell them how much the Lord has done for you, and how he has had mercy on you' (Mark 5:19). It may have been more glorious to accompany Jesus, probably more comforting, and doubtless it would have seemed more 'holy,' but Jesus knew there was something this fellow could do for

Him among his own family. And that matters to Jesus too, even though to us it may seem routine and ordinary.

But that is good news for the believer. Christ's sway engulfs the routine and ordinary, the home front. Jesus rules and cares about all of life; everywhere we are on sacred ground. God rules over all of life: nothing is outside his dominion – whether business and politics, economics and education, science and sex, history and harvests, art and affliction, music and marriage, plumbing and preaching. All of life is holy and must be submitted to his reign.

All the activity of life then is holy turf. And we don't believe we have to be smashingly 'successful' to be 'in God's will.' When you play with your two-year-old, wash dishes, or change the oil, you are doing holy work, namely, the will of Christ. We believe that – at least in our heads.

Now if these are peculiar beliefs and if it would be peculiar to believe such peculiar beliefs, then, we suppose, we are a peculiar people. But at least you know it ahead of time. You can't say we didn't warn you. At least you know the kind of things you will hear in the preaching and teaching of our church. Again, *our* church, speaking loosely.

What Our Church Is

2

'I was finally going to live in the south! So at my first restaurant breakfast in Virginia I ordered grits. But when they came I realized I didn't know what grits were – and therefore didn't know how to 'use' them. Did one pour milk and sprinkle sugar on them – or what? It's important to know what something is; then you might know what to do with it. So with the church.'

Jesus promised, 'I will build my church, and the powers of death shall not prevail against it' (Matt. 16:18). That sounds pretty certain and definite. But just what sort of church did Jesus build? What sort of animal is the church? What is the church according to the Bible? Let's pick up some brief biblical answers from the apostle Paul.

A Bible church

Paul tells us the church is a building. Check out 1 Corinthians 3:1-17. Not a bricks-and-mortar type of building but a flesh-and-blood building. Paul says of Christians: 'you are ... God's building' (v. 9) of which Jesus Christ is the foundation (v. 11). And that building is a temple (vv. 16-17). God's people are 'God's temple.' Now the big characteristic of a temple is that it is 'sacred.' So when Paul describes the church as a temple, he is saying it is fearfully sacred – so sacred that anyone who dares to destroy God's people-temple is headed for deep trouble (vv. 16-17).

But the church is a 'she,' for the church is a bride. See Ephesians 5:22-33. Now everybody should know what a bride's for, and, if they don't, they've no business having one. 'Husbands,' Paul ordered, 'love your wives, just as Christ also loved the church and gave himself for her' (Eph. 5:25). If the church is a bride it means that she is dearly loved. Many griping Christians ought to ape Jesus' attitude toward the church.

But the church, Paul teaches, is also a body (1 Cor. 12:12-26), so that, as with the human body, there is both unity and diversity, and all the various parts are interdependent. Every part of the body needs every other part, no matter how important or insignificant each seems to be. Now if God's people are like that, it means that no one should ever say, 'I don't matter' (vv. 15-17, the attitude of despair). Nor should anyone say, 'I don't need anyone' (v. 21ff, the attitude of pride). A muscular leg might tend to be arrogant until it realizes it is useless without an efficiently working hip. If the church is a body, then Christians are mutually responsible to and for each other's welfare, so that the church is (should be) one place in the world where there is nurture, care, and sympathy for one another.

All the above is very brief, but it should give us some idea of what the Bible has in mind when it speaks of God's people as the 'church,' the house that Jesus built. And it should keep before us a measuring-stick by which to judge our own congregation. Which brings us to the local church. We'll take some time to explain what this is and how it functions.

A local church

Why don't we approach this by picking apart the name of your congregation, starting from the end and working backwards?

Church

What makes a church a church? When is a church really a church rather than a non-church? Must it have a certain number of people attending? Have so much filthy lucre in its treasury? Have a resident pastor or at least three stained-glass windows? What are the marks of a true church?

Usually, we say there are three marks of the church. The first is the preaching of the word. That is the first item noted about the early believers in Jerusalem – 'they devoted themselves to the apostles' teaching' (Acts 2:42). The church is the arena in which God's truth is to be on display (1 Tim. 3:15). A church can only remain a true church so long as it receives God's truth in the scriptures. That is why it is so crucial what a particular church thinks about the Bible. A second mark: the provision of the sacraments, administered and received in the proper manner (Matt. 28:18-20, 1 Cor. 11:23-6), and done because Christ commanded it. Third, the practice of discipline (Heb. 13:17; Matt. 18:15-20), discipline which the elders are charged to exercise in a vigilant, loving, and careful manner, in order to direct the lives of God's people in godliness.

Discipline is not simply negative or a matter of correcting faults or flagrant sins; it is also positive. As one of my friends said, whenever the word of God is preached God's people are under discipline, for they are being called to shape their thoughts and lives to God's requirements.

Presbyterian

Now there's a corker. What does Presbyterian mean? Most people just know it as a word that's hard to spell correctly. What is a Presbyterian Church anyway?

The term refers to how a church is governed; that is, rule by presbyters or elders. (Now you can see why we are called Presbyterian – who ever heard of an elderian church?) There are, actually, two offices in the local church (here you can check 1 Timothy 3:1-13; 5:17-20). The deacons have a serving office intended to display humility before God's people (the deacons' service points to the serving activity all God's people should show); this is needed because God's people are prone to pride. The elders hold a ruling office intended to exercise control over God's people; this is necessary because God's people are prone to wandering (see further on elders, 1 Peter 5:1-4; Hebrews 13:17).

So a Presbyterian Church is one in which there is rule by presbyters or elders. Elders are elected by the people. There are teaching elders (pastors) and ruling elders (cf. 1 Tim. 5:17). They rule with equal authority. Elders of the local church constitute the session. Elders from churches in a region form a presbytery. Elders from churches throughout the nation, and beyond, form the General Assembly.

Reformed

Sneaky, huh? This term is not part of many church's names, but a Presbyterian Church is also a Reformed church.

'Reformed' refers to our doctrine or teaching (whereas 'Presbyterian' refers to the way the church is governed). Our doctrine flows from the Bible – from the faith taught in the Bible and rediscovered in the Protestant Reformation of the sixteenth century. You already have a brief summary of what 'Reformed' doctrine is in chapter one. And these doctrines are summarized in our standards, the *Westminster Confession of Faith* and the Larger and Shorter Catechisms. So we needn't go back over that. But we should consider another question that may be bothering you.

Why do we have – or think we have to have – these 'confessions of faith,' these summations of Bible doctrine? Why don't we just follow the Bible? Good question.

Reason number one: A summary of essential doctrines is very useful (even necessary perhaps). When you want to get a driver's license, why don't the traffic examiners make you go to the courthouse or state capital and study all the various and sundry traffic laws on the books before they allow you to take your driver's test? Well, who knows the answer to that? But you're glad they don't! Instead they give you, for convenience, a small booklet with the main traffic regulations you normally need to know (plus one or six extras). That is very, very helpful. Now that is both unlike and like the relation between the Bible and doctrinal summaries. Unlike, in that we are perfectly happy with having the small traffic booklet and have absolutely no desire ever to read through all the traffic regulations wherever they are; by contrast the Bible itself is always far more interesting and fascinating for the Christian than any human summary of its teaching. But the similarity remains: the Bible does cover a lot of ground and we often are thankful to have this handy digest of its teaching in our confession of faith.

Reason number two: If we have a confession of faith (or doctrinal digest) people can see exactly what we believe. If we were to tell them, 'Why, the Bible is our creed,' then they would have to ask: 'Well, but what do you think the Bible teaches about God's nature, Christ's person, man's need, the sacraments...?' On and on it would go. Now if you have a confession of faith, folks can see precisely what you think the Bible teaches. And it saves everybody a lot of time and painkillers.

You might be asking: Does one have to agree with everything in our confession of faith to unite with our church? No. Our concern is whether you are 'in Christ,' rather than with whether you agree with every jot and tittle of our doctrine. But in our church you should expect to find teaching and thinking like that in the Confession (if that is what the Bible teaches – and we think it is), and if you think you could not stomach that, wisdom suggests that you hold off joining.

Your church's name

Here's where the rubber meets the pew! Here the church is a particular group of believers in a particular place. What can you expect to find in a church? You will probably find...

1. Persons who will disappoint you and sometimes infuriate you. No rosy or even peachy perfection here. It's like being 'on a quest for the perfect cup of coffee.' Not many are on that quest, but some are looking for the perfect church and always coming up disappointed. You must remember that the church is a hospital for sinners. The church is precisely where we sinners need to be, but it can make life pretty trying at times.

2. People who still struggle against sin and are enduring severe trials. Any number of our people

have been through a lot of heavy weather – and the winds are still blowing. That means we may not always be smiling, upbeat people with that 'victorious' air about us (though we trust there is deep gospel joy in us).

3. A church that seeks to worship God carefully and thoughtfully. We try to place a high priority on public worship. Hence we try to plan it carefully. We don't want people simply attending church – we want them adoring God; we don't want them merely coming to a service – we want them entering God's presence. Sometimes worship may seem a bit formal to some, but formal is not the same as dead. If it seems dead, it's probably because you're not worshiping. In any case, we seek to lead people into thinking, joyful, solemn worship that is worthy of God.

4. A diligent effort to provide biblical preaching and teaching that both informs the mind and stirs the feelings. This is to a large degree the task of the teaching elder. Note that the pastor's proper title is 'teaching elder,' for teaching is his primary task. A good bit of pastoring is to be done by all believers as they care for one another.

That is what you can expect – perhaps. Sometimes we'll fail to care for each other as we ought. Sometimes we'll ignore people, so that they feel they don't matter. You may think that this is not a great sales pitch. You're right. It's even worse. We are not even salesmen at all. We are an imperfect body of believers convinced that Jesus loves us in spite of ourselves and seeking to become more faithful to him by becoming more faithful to his people. And you are welcome to become a part of us.

My church?

You may have some questions now.

What if I think I want to join with a body of believers? What procedure do I follow?

Procedures may vary a little from place to place but here is typically what happens in a congregation:

1. Inform a ruling elder or the teaching elder of your intention. No one badgers you to take this step.
2. Typically, two elders will arrange to meet with you. They will want to ask you about

your faith in Christ, your willingness to submit to the oversight of this church and session, and any personal struggles you may be having.

3. Next you would meet with all the elders (session) and, if the way is clear, be received as a member.

What sort of commitment must I make?

When someone confesses (or re-confesses) his or her faith when joining a church, that person enters into a solemn covenant with God and his church. In our denomination when it is someone's first public confession, he or she is asked to affirm the following vows:

1. Do you acknowledge yourself to be a sinner in the sight of God, justly deserving his displeasure, and without hope save [except] in his sovereign mercy?

2. Do you believe in the Lord Jesus Christ as the Son of God, and Savior of sinners, and do you receive and rest upon him alone for salvation as he is offered in the Gospel?

3. Do you now resolve and promise, in humble reliance upon the grace of the Holy Spirit,

that you will endeavor to live as becomes the followers of Christ [that is, in a way that reflects well on Jesus]?

4. Do you promise to support the church in its worship and work to the best of your ability?

5. Do you submit yourself to the government and discipline of the church, and promise to study [seek] its purity and peace?

What is my place in this congregation? Do I have a ministry here?

A good question. However, your ministry may be 'out there' more than 'in here.' Not that there won't be a ministry for you within the church. But we urge you to take a hard look at the place where God has placed you in your weekday life – your daily vocation, your home, your school, whatever. Usually, it seems it pleases God to begin to use us in the calling where he has placed us. Our task is to be a window through which the rays of God's splendor can splash upon our various 'worlds.' And that doesn't mean we have to be a smashing success. For some New Testament Christians it simply meant doing their daily work with all their heart because they were doing it 'for the Lord' and not for men (Col. 3:23). That may be your primary ministry – and the teaching and prayers of God's people in the church may prove the support you need to keep sustaining you in that ministry.

How Christians Live 3

Have you heard of *the means of grace*? The means
of grace refers to the ways God usually uses to
cause Christians to grow and mature in Christ.
The Reformed church has customarily said that
there are three means of grace: the word, the
sacraments, and prayer. Let us discuss these
three instruments God uses and, after that,
look at two more practices which also stimulate
Christian growth.

The Word

You may hear the word of God publicly or
privately. Sometimes you hear the word taught

or preached in the public gatherings of God's people. But you can also hear the word through your personal reading of the Scriptures (or through family study of the Bible). Here we want to focus on the personal reading of Scripture.

Please check out Luke 10:38-42. You should always be careful about opening your home to Jesus because you never know what he will do there. Ask Martha; 'Martha opened her home to him' (v. 38). And the trouble started. Seems Martha had a sister, Mary, 'who sat at the Lord's feet listening to what he said' (v. 39). Now it only takes one casserole to boil over to get hot yourself – especially if you see your sister quietly sitting (of all things) and listening to your dinner guest. Exasperated, Martha blurts at Jesus: 'Lord, don't you care that my sister has left me to do the work by myself? Tell her to help me!' (v. 40). Now when Martha raised all this flak about Mary helping her with salads and casseroles and…, Jesus had an answer: 'Mary has chosen what is better, and it will not be taken away from her' (v. 42).

Now what do we make of all that? Did Martha think Mary should *never* listen to Jesus' teaching? Did she want Jesus to refrain from teaching in her house? No and no. She simply believed that there were times when listening to the word of God must take second place to the pressing needs of the moment. And Jesus? Jesus believed that listening to the word of God must simply become a priority through deliberate neglect if need be (v. 42). 'Mary has chosen what is better' – and he said that before even tasting Martha's meal. Hearing the word of God is more important than having a regular meal. At least Jesus isn't a hypocrite – he had skipped meals before (see Luke 4:1-4).

How much time should I spend?

Well, let me make some suggestions about daily Bible reading. To begin with, I wouldn't spend more than ten to fifteen minutes in reading and thinking over a portion of Scripture. That may disappoint you. You may have expected me to say that you 'really need to get into the word' and to suggest some astronomical time frame so that you could feel appropriately guilty and think it utterly impossible. No, I don't think that is the way. I am more satisfied to see Christians with consistent hunger than periodic gluttony. When should this time be? Whenever it's best for you. Some people are more alert in the mornings, some in the evenings. Some may find time and solitude over lunch hour. Just one thing: more often than not you'll have to make time. If it's breakfast or Bible, you skip breakfast. If it's lunch or the Lord, too bad for lunch. You must make time. Get up fifteen minutes earlier in the morning (which may mean you must go to bed earlier at night). Or whatever. But you must plot and conspire and sabotage to have this time. It seldom comes naturally. Ask Martha.

Where should I begin?

When first starting out I would not suggest reading straight through the Bible; start with the Gospel of Mark. After that you could try 1 John, then Genesis, Luke, and then go back to Exodus 1–20. That will give you a start.

What do I do when I read?

What should I look for? Look for something in the Bible passage which you can use for that day. Maybe it shows you something about God or Christ that leads you to worship or praise. Maybe it provides correction you need for an attitude or habit. Maybe it brings assurance to you in some anxiety or fear.

Let's take the time for several examples. Say you are reading in Mark 1:1-13. Now you come to verse 11 and you read that when Jesus was baptized the voice from heaven said: 'You are my Son, whom I love; with you I am well pleased.' Then what? Then the Spirit sends Jesus out into the desert 'and he was in the desert forty days being tempted by Satan' (v. 13). Now maybe you notice that. Jesus receives this wonderful assurance in verse 11, then he is plunged into temptation in verse 13. The two are side-by-side. As you ponder that, doesn't a point hit you? The fact that you are being sorely tempted (or tried) does not mean that God is displeased with you. That may sound like little. But it's worth meditating on, for when you are in the throes of temptation it is almost automatic to think that God is surely displeased with you. Here, if you will think about it, is wonderful assurance for dark times.

Pretend you are reading Mark 1:14-28. And you happen on those words that the unclean spirit shrieked at Jesus in verse 24: 'What do you want with us, Jesus of Nazareth? Have you come to destroy us? I know who you are – the Holy One of God!' Think about that. A demon has correct knowledge about Jesus. 'You are the Holy One of God.' Since it is a demon that speaks, we know that this knowledge he has is not a *saving* knowledge or a *loving* knowledge. But he knows truth about Jesus. Should this not bring us up short and make us examine ourselves? It should make me say, 'Why, even demons have a certain kind of "faith". Is that all *my* faith is – knowing or confessing certain facts about Jesus? Does my faith go beyond a demonic "faith"?' And so you turn this Scripture on your own insides and scrutinize yourself; you examine yourself.

Then the next day you are reading Mark 1:29-39 (sure, it takes a while to go through a chapter this way, but what's the hurry?). And you read about Jesus & Co. going to Simon and Andrew's home after synagogue service. Now Simon's (that is, Peter's) mother-in-law 'lay sick with a fever, and immediately they told him of her' (v. 30). That is very simple – it's elementary school level. But so what? Doesn't that provide you with some instruction? What can you do better in face of trouble or sickness or distress, whenever it comes, than to tell Jesus about it? What is *your* first resort in trouble? Do you tell him? Where have you been taking your troubles recently? Do you see how simply turning the Bible in on yourself can lead you to see your own failures and your true comfort?

Next day you are finishing Mark 1, reading verses 40-5. Here is this man with leprosy standing in front of Jesus. And Jesus shocks you, for 'he stretched out his hand and touched him' (v. 41). Now lepers were 'unclean' and therefore cut off from normal society. That man had probably not felt a human touch in years. A leper. Jesus touched him. Does that tell you anything about the kind of Savior you have? Without drawing out the implications any more, can you see how – if you continued to ponder those words and that scene, how you would be forced to fall at Jesus' feet in wonder, love, and praise, and worship such a Lord who doesn't flinch from touching filthy people like us? Well, there are fifteen more chapters in Mark but we must move on.

The sacraments

What are the sacraments? Baptism and the Lord's Supper. All right, but what makes a sacrament a sacrament? A sacrament is a sacrament when it is an action (1) instituted by Christ (see Matt. 28:18-20 for baptism and 1 Cor. 11:23-6 on the Lord's Supper), (2) which he intended to be observed repeatedly, (3) among all God's people. Item three (among all God's people) is why we do not regard such things as marriage or 'holy orders' as sacraments – they don't apply to all God's people.

But what, really, is a 'sacrament'? John Calvin put it this way: A sacrament is an outward symbol by which the Lord seals in our consciences the promises of his good will toward us, to sustain the weakness of our faith. That is, sacraments are God's authorized illustrations to prop up our weak faith. Sacraments are given not to make God's promises more sure but to make *us* more sure of God's promises. (That's what Calvin meant when he said that the Lord by a sacrament 'seals in our consciences the promises of his good will toward us').

So how is this process supposed to work? Suppose you are a Christian and beset with nagging doubts about whether the Lord really has cleansed your sins away. Ever have doubts, gnawing doubts, about that? You think back on your baptism. You should then begin to think like this: Just as the water used in baptism cleanses the body, so just as surely God has cleansed me of every spot. Or suppose a Christian comes to the Lord's Supper and he or she is going through a grievous affliction at the time, and with it – as often happens – begins to wonder if the Lord has cast him off or has forsaken her. When such struggling Christians receive the bread and the wine, it is as if Jesus says to them: 'You see, if I went this far for you in your sins, do you think I will cast you off in your trials?' (e.g. Rom. 8:32).

But how does that assurance come with the sacrament? By faith. Sounds like a cop-out, doesn't it? After all, it seems strange that common items like water or bread and wine could ever assure anyone. How can such things assure us of God's faithfulness? Let's look at it this way...

When you shop for groceries you may have green beans on the list. Maybe three cans. How do you know when you reach for that particular can that you have green beans? Ah, you say, I see this label with this picture of green beans on it (admit it: you trust the label). Now if all the cans on the shelves were stripped of their labels and appeared in all their tinny glory and there was a grocery clerk stationed on the aisle to tell you – when you asked – which were the green beans, well, that should work. But don't you *feel* more sure of getting green beans when you see the can in its usual dress, wearing its green and blue and red label? In one way there's no sense to it, but somehow you feel more sure of what you're getting if the can carries the label than if a clerk merely points out which bare cans have green beans in them. Somehow, the label 'brings home' to you the conviction that you really have green beans. That is the way the sacraments work. There is something about seeing Christ's pictures that assures us of his love. So the sacraments press into our souls the conviction that God's goodness and mercy really *will* follow us all the days of our life – and more besides.

Prayer

If you are a Christian you will pray. Or at least Jesus thought so. When Jesus taught on prayer he began, 'When you pray, do not be like the hypocrites' (Matt. 6:5). Did you note that? 'When you pray...' Jesus takes it for granted that his disciples will pray. You could turn that around. You could say that if someone doesn't pray, he or she must not be Jesus' disciple.

Now Jesus also teaches his disciples how to pray. That's what Matthew 6:5-15 is all about, particularly the 'Lord's Prayer' in verses 9-13. Remember how it begins? 'Our Father...' That means prayer is not for everybody. Only for Jesus' disciples, only for those who have come to God through Jesus (John 1:12; 14:6). But those two words also tell us that prayer is intimate. We come to God as children to a father. (Note: when Jesus refers to God as Father, he means 'Father' in the best sense of that word, of all that a father should be; see Matt. 7:9-11).

In the Lord's Prayer you will notice a certain pattern: God's name, God's kingdom, God's will; and then our food, our forgiveness, our security. God's interests come before our needs.

Not that our needs don't count. But we should be more concerned about God's worship and will than our needs and desires. That's one way you 'seek first his kingdom' (Matt. 6:33). But we do have needs and Jesus teaches us to pray about them. We have anxiety so we pray for provision (daily bread); we have guilt so we pray for pardon (forgive sins); we have weakness so we pray for protection (from the evil one).

Why don't you step back and look over the whole Lord's Prayer? What about how short it is? Prayer doesn't have to be long, drawn out, and last a half-hour. What about how simple it is? These requests are not expressed in some special 'prayer language,' complete with 'thou couldst' or 'shouldst' – nor are there any seven syllable words. So you don't have to make a B+ in English before you can talk to your Father. I suggest that you keep your prayers like this – short, simple, and – let's add, secret (Matt. 6:6). Not that you never pray in public; but spend some time in secret with your heavenly Father each day in some place where you won't normally be interrupted. Speak to him simply – you don't need to impress your Father with your extensive vocabulary or your fine turn of phrase. And keep it pretty short; after all, you can speak to your Father all through the day, so you don't need to bring up everything at once. After all, to call God 'our Father' means that prayer is the expression of a relationship. And if we've a close relationship with someone, we surely will want to talk with that person frequently, all through the day.

Worship

I am not referring to private worship but especially to public worship in the assembly of God's people.

Worship is a hot topic in the church right now – some say we are fighting the 'worship wars.' I will not enlist in a war just now but Christians should be alert to certain distortions of worship.

The entertainment model

The driving passion in such 'worship' is that people enjoy themselves. Church should be pleasant. Out with the glum, in with the sun. Armed with microphones and amplifiers, a praise team may lead the singing. Nothing wrong with a little electricity. But a subtle shift can take place: performance can replace participation. The preacher in this scheme is primarily a 'communicator' seeking to bring immediate help to an area of felt need rather than explaining and applying a biblical text. Being upbeat is what matters.

A new church once sent out an e-mail to a database of Christians in its area. It was offering a 'non-judgmental atmosphere.' Now that's better than a judgmental one. But if it means the church intends to be so positive that it will never disturb anyone, then we have a sad affair on our hands. Such churches and such worship assume they exist to sustain their people's happiness.

The service station model

Here the worshiper views worship as the place (clinic?) to get his or her needs met. Now don't go ballistic. God does care about the needs of his people: he is near to the broken-hearted and saves the crushed in spirit. But if we navel-gaze on our needs, if we begin there, then we are going to be consumers rather than worshipers and will prefer to use God rather than adore him.

The lecture hall model

This can be common in churches that have a high view of the preaching-teaching ministry. Out come the pencils and notebooks. The assumption is that worship consists mainly, nearly only, in learning; all the prayers, hymns, and confessions of faith are merely the 'preliminaries.' What really matters is amassing Bible teaching, Bible knowledge, Bible content, Bible principles from an authoritative preacher or teacher.

The problem with these approaches to worship is that they are all 'me-centered' (which means that they are idolatrous). The entertainment model focuses on my enjoyment, the service station model on my needs, and the lecture hall model on my learning. But worship is not about me – it's about God!

This is why we must be careful here. To say that you will grow as a Christian through the worship of God is a bit dangerous or misleading, for it may lead someone to think that the main reason you worship is in order to grow as a

Christian. That is not it at all. The reason you should worship is because God ought to be worshiped, whether it 'does' anything for you or not. We worship God because God has commanded us to do so (e.g. Pss. 95 & 100) and because he is worthy of all praise. Let's be blunt. That's part of the problem in contemporary Christianity. God is viewed as a wonderful Vending Machine in the Clouds, and if we put the right things into him (it?), we get the goodies. In this way of thinking, we worship God because it makes us feel better, when the truth is we should worship God because he deserves our praise – whether we feel better or not.

So, as far as worship is concerned, seek to develop a hunger for God himself. 'As the deer pants for streams of water, so my soul pants for you, O God. My soul thirsts for God, for the living God. When can I go and meet with God?' (Ps. 42:1-2). 'O God, you are my God, earnestly I seek you; my soul thirsts for you, my body longs for you, in a dry and weary land where there is no water' (Ps. 63:1). 'How lovely is your dwelling place, O LORD of hosts! My soul yearns, even faints for the courts of the LORD; my heart and my flesh cry out for the living God' (Ps. 84:1-2). So we seek God for himself and not merely for his benefits.

But, having said that, we must also say that the God we meet in worship is a God who revels in loading us with benefits. That's why Psalm 84 can describe those whose hearts cry out for the living God as ones who also 'go from strength to strength' (Ps. 84:7). You will frequently find that to be so: as you seek God for his own sake he will strengthen, sustain, and put fresh heart into you. There is that strange chemistry in public worship. It is there, as you wallow in the word, sacraments, and prayer, that God stoops down and puts fresh heart into his faltering people.

Fellowship

That is, unfortunately, a mushy word. What is fellowship? The word is so vague nowadays that it is used to describe the pot-luck supper at the Firemen's Hall, or the great time everyone had mixing at the county fair, or any time when we get the warm fuzzies with other people. In western culture fellowship seems to be equated with any occasion involving food.

But you don't have fellowship at the PTA. Fellowship is not mere camaraderie. In the Bible, fellowship is the communion-relationship we have with God the Father and with Jesus Christ (see 1 John 1:3); and when we have that intimate relationship with Christ it also brings us into fellowship with all Christ's people ('fellowship with one another,' 1 John 1:7). If God is our Father through Jesus then all his children are our brothers and sisters; that is, we are part of a family, of a 'household.' You may remember what the Pittsburgh Pirates called themselves in 1979, when they whipped the Baltimore Orioles in the World Series: 'We are family.' That should be especially true of the church.

And it is true – at least according to the Bible. In 1 Timothy 3:15 Paul calls the church 'God's household', and so the church is God's family. If so, we should be eager to spend more time with our brothers and sisters. 'Let us not give up meeting together, as some are in the habit of doing, but let us encourage one another – and all the more as you see the Day approaching' (Heb. 10:25). That seems to mean that one place (or time) where we meet other 'family' members is in the worship assemblies of the church.

Part of that time should consist of 'encouraging one another', which, one assumes, takes place through study of the Scriptures and mutual prayer (Rom. 15:4; Eph. 6:18; cf. Col. 3:16), as well as holy conversation. God intends other believers to be channels of his encouragement and strength to you (and you to them). Fellowship is vital. If a coal burns by itself it will go out; but if it is heaped together with other burning coals it will go on burning.

Growth comes from God (1 Cor. 3:6-7). But God has 'means of grace' through which he usually brings growth, established channels by which his strength comes to us. The grace is God's, but we are to use the means. We are to be 'on the grow.' Or, to put it better: 'But grow in the grace and knowledge of our Lord and Savior Jesus Christ' (2 Pet. 3:18).

The Matter that Matters

4

It was a direct question. 'Who do you say I am?' (Matt. 16:15). There was no side-stepping Jesus' question to his disciples. And he is just as direct with us. What are we going to say about Jesus? What are we going to do with him? Nothing more important than that. But first we should remember what he has done for us.

Guilty

Now remember who you are. The apostle has written your biography in Romans 3:10-18.

I know – you don't think that really describes you. It's just a bunch of Old Testament quotes about really bad people, you say. But the apostle won't budge. No, he says, apart from Christ that is a description of you (and v. 19 says that these things were spoken to religious people). So, I am guilty, that is, I am under the penalty of sin.

We may say, 'Well, big deal. Why doesn't God just forgive sin?' But can God 'just forgive'? Think of the murderer before the judge. The judge tears up, wipes his eyes, and then says that he has decided to overlook the murderer's crime and to 'forgive' him. Now that would upset some people. After all, what about the guy's victims? The judge can't 'just forgive' him – that would make a mockery of justice. When God forgives our sins it doesn't mean he simply overlooks them. He must forgive sins righteously, justly. Somewhere, somehow, the penalty for sin must be paid. The good news is that the Judge himself has paid the penalty in the person of his Son. Let's get at it via a story that P. T. Forsyth once told about a man named Shamel who was fighting against the Czarist regime in Russia about 1870:

His was a guerilla group, including not only the fighting men but also their families and their livestock... His organization was his own little universe, with laws fundamental to its own existence. Then one day stealing broke out in his camp and his organization began to fall apart in mutual suspicion. So Shamel laid down the law and announced the penalty. 'Thou shalt not steal,' and the penalty was one hundred lashes. Before long the thief was caught. But it was Shamel's own mother! Now he had the problem of law and love. For the sake of his universe the law must stand; in no society can stealing be treated with indifference. At the same time he loved his mother and could not face the requirements of his own law that she should bear the one hundred lashes. Who could see his own mother bear such a beating? Shamel shut himself in his own tent for three days trying to find his solution and finally came out with his mind made up; his mother, for the sake of the law and for the sake of the whole society, must receive the lashes. How many societies have failed because at this very point they could not hold to the law! But before three blows had fallen Shamel had his real and final solution, his revelation. He removed his mother from her penalty and required that they lay on his own back the full measure of every blow. The price had to be paid in full, but the price was paid by him. His law stood; his love stood. The only possible solution was to receive the punishment in his own person.

As told by Addison H. Leitch
Interpreting Basic Theology

Did you catch that? 'The only possible solution was to receive the punishment in his own person.' That's how God works forgiveness – he received the punishment in the person of his Son, who 'was pierced through for our rebellions, he was crushed for our iniquities; the punishment that brought us peace was upon him' (Isa. 53:5).

Dirty

There is another picture of us – including you – in the Bible. I am not only guilty but I am dirty, I am filthy, I am covered with the pollution of sin. That's why David prayed, 'Wash away all my iniquity and cleanse me from my sin' (Ps. 51:2) and why Paul says Christ gave himself for us 'to purify for himself a people' (Titus 2:14). Sin defiles and we must know the right way to get washed.

When I was a boy about six or seven years old I decided I would do my father a big favor and wash the car (something my father rarely, if ever, did). So I got me a bucket, filled it maybe half-way with water, located an old dirty rag in the garage, dipped my rag in the bucket, and wiped it all over the car as high as I could reach. I used no hose, did no rinsing, just kept dipping my rag in the bucket. Strangely enough, when the car (which was black) was dry, it was covered with swirls of a sort of mud glaze (or haze – who knows?). It looked horrendous! My way of washing washed nothing. Now I was very sincere. But that didn't matter – the car looked hideous.

That is a parable of any of our own attempts to cleanse ourselves of sin. Rather, 'the blood of Jesus, his Son, keeps cleansing us from every sin' (1 John 1:7).

And when Jesus cleanses us we are really cleansed – *no matter how filthy we have been.* Some people simply cannot believe this. But what does the word of God say? Try this:

> Don't you know that the wicked will not inherit the kingdom of God? Do not be deceived: Neither the sexually immoral nor idolaters nor adulterers nor male prostitutes nor homosexual offenders nor thieves nor the greedy nor drunkards nor slanderers nor swindlers will inherit the kingdom of God. And that is what some of you were. But you were washed… (1 Cor. 6:9-11a).

What do you say to that? Did Christ only do that for sinners at Corinth in the first century? Doesn't that show you that there is no stain too deep or lurid but that the blood of Jesus can totally erase it?

Enslaved

Let me show you a third picture that the Bible gives of us as sinners. It says that we are enslaved and that we are under the power of sin. Paul puts it briefly: all men, whether religious or pagan, are 'under sin' (Rom. 3:9). He means that they are, as the Revised Standard Version translates it, 'under the power of sin.' Most people probably don't think that way about sin. Many people think of sin as something they do or fail to do. But Paul quite often speaks of sin as power, a strong force that holds you in its grip. You may not understand it – for it is mysterious. Still, it is real.

I recall an incident when I was about ten years old. We lived in a small western Pennsylvania town where my father was the United Presbyterian pastor. Now a new Methodist pastor named Rev. Galbraith moved to town. His wife was, quite predictably, Mrs Galbraith. They were a friendly and cordial couple and became good friends with my parents. However, bashful as I was, I failed to speak to Mrs Galbraith on one or two occasions. Hence she teasingly threatened that if I didn't speak to her when she saw me next, she would kiss me. Sheer, unmitigated terror! No problem, you say. All you have to do is henceforth to speak to her. Oh? You don't understand that such jesting threats induce a kind of social paralysis on ten-year-olds. Mysterious it is. But for some inexplicable reason one simply 'can't' speak to a woman who threatens to smooch you if you don't speak. It was so bad that when three of our local churches had our weekly Sunday evening services together, I would dash out of church immediately after the service to avoid having to face Mrs Galbraith. No see, no kiss. It got worse. Once when (after evening church) I was sitting in our family car, Mrs G. and her husband were walking home. She came toward the car to speak to me, but, fearing what might be coming, I jumped out of the car on the street-traffic side, almost into the path of an on-coming auto, obviously preferring a tragic – rather than a romantic – end to my life!

Now I cannot explain that. I cannot state why I didn't just speak to her and 'be free.' All I know is that, ludicrous as it sounds, I could not speak to her! I was enslaved. I was in bondage. I was helpless in the grip of that threat.

That is what Paul means when he says you are 'under sin.' Sin is a tyrant that holds you tightly in its grip and you have no hope unless the Strong Son of God wrenches you from its clutches. That Jesus has done, especially in his death. That's why John can speak of Jesus as 'the one who loves us and has set us free from our sins at the cost of his blood' (Rev. 1:5).

That is what Jesus has done for his people. We are guilty, dirty, and enslaved, subject to the penalty, pollution, and power of sin. From all this, Christ's death releases us.

Are you ready to come?

Back to the original question. What will you do with him? What have you done with him? Jesus said: 'All that the Father gives me will come to me, and whoever comes to me I will never cast out' (John 6:37). That is basically what faith is – coming to Christ. See how he encourages you - whoever comes, he says, 'I will never cast out.' You are assured of a glad welcome. Have you 'come' to him? Then the benefits of Jesus' death will be applied to you.

But wait! Don't come yet. Do you understand what you are getting into? Aha, you say, I thought there was a catch! Wrong. No catch. But a cost. And it's all Jesus' fault. Well, he said it: 'Anyone who loves father or mother more than me is not worthy of me; anyone who loves son or daughter more than me is not worthy of me; and anyone who does not take his cross and follow after me is not worthy of me' (Matt. 10:37-8). You see, don't you, what Jesus requires? He is saying that he demands the place of supreme affection in your life. Are you ready to surrender that? And what about this 'cross'? The cross meant one thing to a first-century Jew – it was the way Romans put criminals to death. Now Jesus says that you must take your cross and follow him, that is, you must be ready, if need be, to die for him.

Just as well give you the whole story. 'You will be hated by all on account of my name' (Mark 13:13). Yes, Jesus said that too. It doesn't matter why the world hates Jesus' disciples; it just does. There's a Peanuts cartoon in which a boy is sitting with a girl on some steps by the sidewalk. Charlie Brown is coming down the street. The boy says, 'Well! Here comes ol' Charlie Brown.' Charlie passes right in front of them and the boy continues: 'Good ol' Charlie Brown ... yes, sir!' Charlie passes completely by. Then the kid says: 'Good ol' Charlie Brown.... How I hate him!' That is the way the pagan machine will react to you, sooner or later, Jesus tells you. 'You will be hated by all on account of my name, *but he who endures to the end will be saved*' (Mark 13:13).

Now are you ready to come? Have you come? Will you come? That's the bottom line. That's the matter that matters.